3105 2052

S0-AEW-858

WITHDRAWN
BEAVERTON CITY LIBRARY
Beaverton, OR 97005
Member of Washington County
COOPERATIVE LIBRARY SERVICES

Picture the Past

Life in Colonial Boston

Jennifer Blizin Gillis

Heinemann Library
Chicago, Illinois

© 2003 Heinemann Library
a division of Reed Elsevier Inc.
Chicago, Illinois
Customer Service 888-454-2279
Visit our website at www.heinemannlibrary.com

All rights reserved. No part of this publication may be
reproduced or transmitted in any form or by any means,
electronic or mechanical, including photocopying,
recording, taping, or any information retrieval system,
without permission in writing from the publisher.

Produced for Heinemann Library by
   Bender Richardson White.
Editor: Lionel Bender
Designer and Media Conversion: Ben White
Picture Researcher: Cathy Stastny
Production Controller: Kim Richardson

07 06 05 04 03
10 9 8 7 6 5 4 3 2 1

Printed and bound by Lake Book Manufacturing, Inc.

Library of Congress Cataloging-in-Publication Data.
Gillis, Jennifer Blizin, 1950-
   Life in colonial Boston / Jennifer Blizin Gillis.
     p. cm. -- (Picture the past)
Summary: An overview of everyday life in the busy port
city of Boston between 1760 and 1773, including the
changes that came as colonists began to resent the
trade restrictions and taxes imposed upon them by
England. Includes bibliographical references and index.
   ISBN 1-4034-3795-5 -- ISBN 1-4034-4284-3 (pbk.)
   1. Boston (Mass.)--History--Colonial period, ca. 1600-1775--
Juvenile
literature. 2. Boston (Mass.)--Social life and customs--18th
century--Juvenile literature. (1. Boston (Mass.)--History--
Colonial period, ca. 1600-1775. 2. Boston (Mass.)--Social life
and customs--18th century.) I. Title. II. Series.
   F73.4.G54 2003
   974.4'6102--dc21
                                        2003005404

Special thanks to Angela McHaney Brown at Heinemann
Library for editorial and design guidance and direction.

Acknowledgments
The producers and publishers are grateful to the following
for permission to reproduce copyright material:
Corbis Images: pp. 7, 16; Angelo Hornak, 17; Lee
Snider/Lee Snider, 18; Burstein Collection, p. 1; Kevin
Fleming, p. 30. North Wind Pictures, p. 22. Peter Newark's
American Pictures, p. 14. The Bridgeman Art Library:
Lauros/Giraudon, p. 9; Library of Congress, Washington
D.C., U.S.A., pp. 24, 25; Massachussetts Historical Society,
cover and pp. 10, 26; Museum of Fine Arts, Boston,
Massachusetts, U.S.A., p. 13; Private collection, p. 29; The
Bayou Bend Collection, gift of Miss Ima Hogg, pp. 11, 12;
Victoria and Albert Museum, London, U.K., p. 15; Worcester
Art Museum, Massachusetts, U.S.A., p. 20; Yale University Art
Gallery, New Haven, C.T., U.S.A., pp. 3, 28.

Maps: Stefan Chabluk
Illustrations: Nick Hewetson, p. 21; John James, pp. 4, 11, 19,
23; Gerald Wood, pp. 6, 26.

Every effort has been made to contact copyright holders
of any material reproduced in this book. Omissions will be
rectified in subsequent printings if notice is given to the
publisher.

ABOUT THIS BOOK

This book tells about life in Boston, Massachusetts, from 1760 to 1773. Boston was one of the largest cities in the thirteen **colonies** of **Great Britain.** At first, the people who lived in Boston copied the way things were done in Britain. But as time passed, they grew unhappy with the fact that they did not make their own laws. By the 1760s, Bostonians felt they were paying too many **taxes** to Britain. They felt they had no say in how their colony was being run. The way people in colonial Boston lived their lives began to show that they wanted to be **independent.**

We have illustrated the book with paintings and drawings from colonial times and with artists' ideas of how things looked then.

The Author

Jennifer Blizin Gillis is an editor and author of nonfiction books and poetry for children. She graduated with a B.A. from Guilford College with a degree in French Literature and Art History. She has taught foreign language and social studies at middle schools in North Carolina, Virginia, and Illinois.

Note to the Reader

Some words are shown in bold, **like this.** You can find out what they mean by looking in the glossary.

CONTENTS

Boston Begins

The town of Boston began when a **colony** was founded at the mouth of the Charles River, on Massachusetts Bay. The **settlers** gave the new town the name of the town where they had lived in **Great Britain**—Boston. They were **Puritans** who wanted freedom to practice their **religion.** At first, the settlers made their own laws. But in 1686, the king sent a governor to Boston, and it became a royal colony. By 1750, about 20,000 people lived there, and it was one of the most important cities in the thirteen American colonies.

Look for these
The illustration of a boy and girl of colonial times shows you the subject of each two-page story in the book.

The illustration of the front of Faneuil Hall marks boxes with interesting facts about life in colonial Boston.

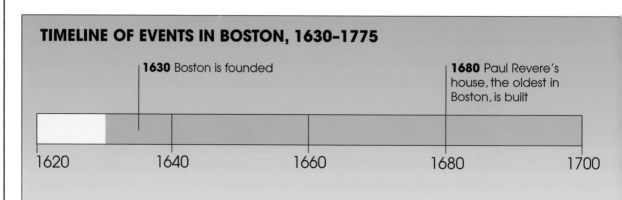

TIMELINE OF EVENTS IN BOSTON, 1630–1775

1630 Boston is founded

1680 Paul Revere's house, the oldest in Boston, is built

1620   1640   1660   1680   1700

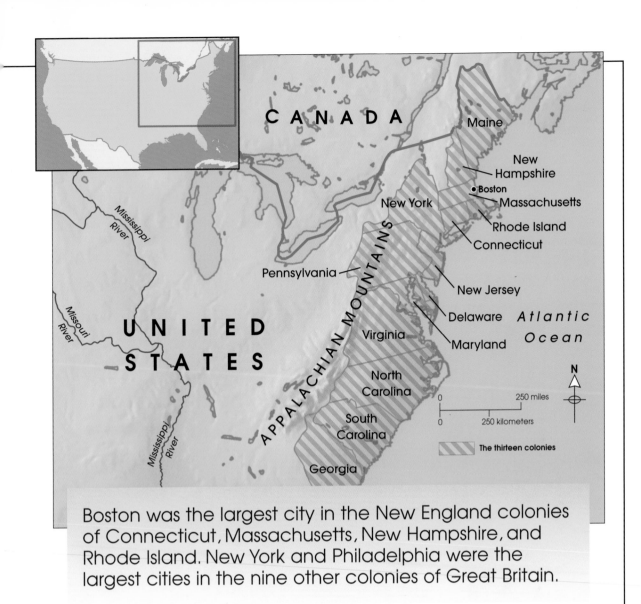

Boston was the largest city in the New England colonies of Connecticut, Massachusetts, New Hampshire, and Rhode Island. New York and Philadelphia were the largest cities in the nine other colonies of Great Britain.

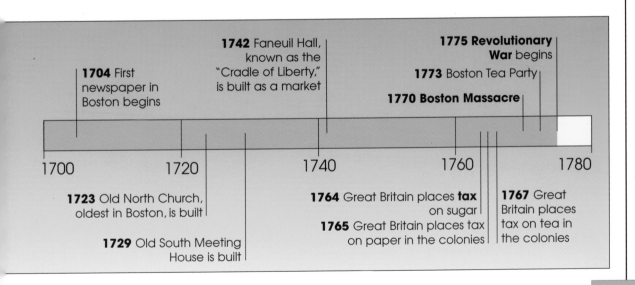

1704 First newspaper in Boston begins

1742 Faneuil Hall, known as the "Cradle of Liberty," is built as a market

1775 Revolutionary War begins

1773 Boston Tea Party

1770 Boston Massacre

1700　　　　1720　　　　1740　　　　1760　　　　1780

1723 Old North Church, oldest in Boston, is built

1729 Old South Meeting House is built

1764 Great Britain places **tax** on sugar

1765 Great Britain places tax on paper in the colonies

1767 Great Britain places tax on tea in the colonies

Busy Port

British officials collected gold from merchant ships as a tax on goods transported through Boston Harbor.

Boston Harbor was a crowded seaport. Ships loaded with lumber, dried fish, or dried beef left for **Great Britain** or other **colonies.** Other ships arrived, filled with goods from Britain and bringing **immigrants** from other countries. Stores around the harbor sold rope, lanterns, candles, and other things needed for ocean voyages. Taverns were filled with sailors and workers.

By law, ships from the colonies could trade only with Great Britain or British colonies. **Colonists** had to pay **taxes** to Great Britain on goods brought to the colonies. But many merchants avoided paying taxes by **smuggling.** They secretly shipped and sold things to other countries and their colonies.

This picture of Boston Harbor shows many ships coming and going. By the mid-1700s, nearly 2,000 ships were going back and forth between Great Britain and the colonies every year.

PETER FANEUIL

Peter Faneuil was a wealthy merchant who gave some of his money to build Boston's Faneuil Hall. This is a list of some of the things he imported, or brought into the country, for his family:
- silk stockings
- candlesticks
- table silver
- razors
- eyeglasses
- cookbooks

Rich Town

Boston grew quickly. Visitors arriving by boat saw a hilly town filled with buildings and church steeples. At first, homes and businesses were side by side. Later, wealthy merchants built large brick homes on a hill above the port. The narrow, winding streets were paved with round stones called cobblestones. Store windows displayed the latest things from **Great Britain.** People shopped at the public market in Faneuil Hall.

Colonists held many meetings at the Town House —seen here on the left—and at the Old South Meeting House. They discussed how they could stop their unfair treatment by the British.

The Old State House in Boston was built in 1713. Here colonial leaders met to try and find a way to free the New England **colonies** from Great Britain.

A VISITOR TO BOSTON

In 1725, a visitor from London wrote: "A gentleman from London would almost think himself at home in Boston when he observes the numbers of people, their houses, their furniture, their tables, their dress and conversation, which perhaps are as splendid and showy as those of the most considerable tradesmen in London."

Wealthy merchants gave money to build churches and other buildings for all the people of Boston. But they had a problem: **taxes.** Although the merchants had to pay taxes to Great Britain, they had no say in how their laws were made. The new churches and buildings became places where angry **colonists** got together to complain about unfair taxes and laws.

Jobs

Craftspeople made many of the things people used in the **colonies.** It often took more than one person to make something. So, craftspeople had **apprentices** who helped them. One of the most important jobs was that of the barrelmaker. Most of what the **colonists** ate, drank, or shipped was stored in barrels.

Tinsmiths also had an important job. Many things people used were made of a soft metal called tin. Carpenters, furniture makers, cabinetmakers, papermakers, printers, bricklayers, and builders also worked in Boston.

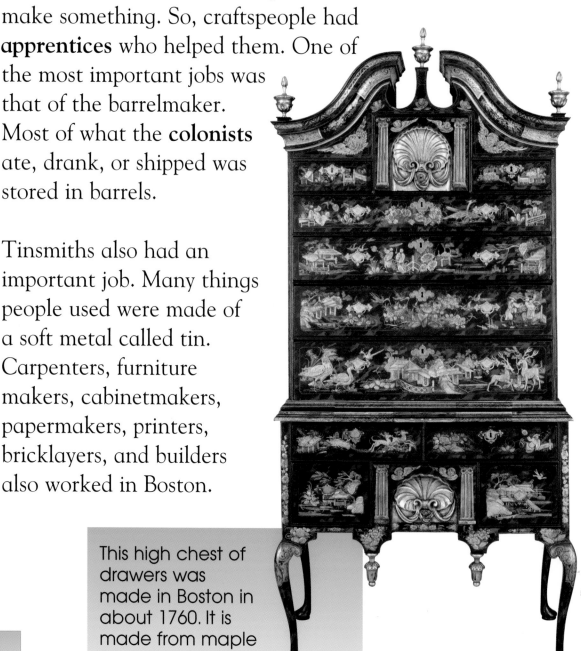

This high chest of drawers was made in Boston in about 1760. It is made from maple and pine wood.

In the 1700s, people usually did not buy things that were already made. If they needed a silver coffeepot, they ordered one from the silversmith. The smith made the coffeepot in the shop, with the help of apprentices.

It was hard to make a living doing just one kind of work. So, many craftspeople did other, similar work. Paul Revere, who was famous for his loyalty to his country, was a silversmith. He was also a printer and goldsmith.

Women had businesses, too. They worked as tavernkeepers, dressmakers, and hatmakers. If a businessman died, his wife could take over his business.

INDENTURED SERVANT

Workers who could not pay for the trip from their country to Boston could become indentured servants. An indentured servant worked for a businessperson or family for a certain amount of time. In return, the businessperson or family paid for the servant's trip to Boston.

Children

Working parents expected their children to get a job as soon as they could. Parents often chose the jobs for their children. Many children became **apprentices** when they were about fourteen years old. They lived with a **craftsperson** and learned everything about the job. Apprentices worked from early in the morning until dark. They could not leave their jobs without the craftsperson's permission.

COLONIAL GAMES

In Great Britain, children played a game of tag in which they had to touch a piece of iron to be "safe." But in Boston, there was more wood and stone than iron. Stone-tag and wood-tag, in which players could tag either stone or wood, took the place of iron-tag. In winter, children played snow-tag.

A son of a wealthy merchant would be trained to work in the family business.

Children from wealthy families had an easier life. They had more time to play games, such as outdoor bowling or hopscotch. They took music and dance lessons. They could spend time reading books or going to parties.

Most children were treated like small adults. They were expected to be seen and not heard, to stay clean, to respect their teachers, and to be polite.

In a wealthy Boston family, children wore clothes similar to those of adults.

Schools

Children from wealthy families went to different schools to learn different things. There were schools for writing, for reading, for music, and for dancing. If a boy was a good student, he could go on to learn Latin, Greek, and mathematics.

Girls learned to read, write, and sew. A girl from a wealthy family might also have lessons in music, dancing, and art.

Children learned to read from books called primers. Primers contained rhymes and poems about people and stories from the Bible.

A   *In Adam's Fall*
    We finned all.

B   *Thy Life to mend;*
    This Book attend.

C   *The Cat doth play,*
    And after flay.

D   *A Dog will bite*
    A Thief at night.

E   *An Eagle's flight*
    Is out of fight.

F   *The idle Fool*
    Is whipt at fchool.

Many teachers gave lessons at their homes or someone else's home. By law, a **craftsperson** had to teach **apprentices** how to read, write, and do arithmetic. If the craftsperson could not teach these lessons, the apprentices went to school a few evenings each week.

Girls were taught fancy sewing stitches. They made a sampler to show off the different stitches. Most of the samplers showed the letters of the alphabet, the girl's name, and a small picture.

Homes

Most **craftspeople** and poor people lived in wooden homes. The top floors hung out over the bottom floors to provide more room upstairs. Windows were small, so the insides of these houses were dark. The downstairs might have just one large room in which the family cooked, ate, and entertained visitors. Upstairs there were one or two rooms to sleep in.

IN SECRET

Many meetings were held in the homes of wealthy people. While men argued and complained about **taxes** in the parlor, or living room, women met in another room to make homemade cloth called homespun.

The house where Paul Revere lived was built for a wealthy merchant in 1680. It was a fine structure for its time. It is the oldest house still standing in Boston.

Wealthy people hired builders to copy the latest styles of buildings in **Great Britain.** Their homes were large and usually made of brick and stone. They had many windows of clear glass, so that the home had more light inside. The kitchen was away from the rest of the house, and most rooms had fireplaces for heat.

This large house in Cambridge, close to Boston, was built in 1759. It was built for Colonel John Vassal. The house has brick chimneys and a painted clapboard surface.

Free Time

FESTIVE LIGHTS

Fireworks and illuminations were popular. Illuminations were large paper decorations that were coated in oil and placed in a park or garden. Candles were lit inside them. After dark, people would stroll around looking at the decorations.

Many men in Boston spent their free time in coffeehouses or taverns. They could meet there to play cards or listen to music. Worries about **taxes** brought wealthy merchants and **craftspeople** from different backgrounds together. They met to discuss what could be done about **Great Britain.**

These designs by Paul Revere show people who collected taxes. The drawings were the four sides of an illuminated obelisk.

Women visited each other at home or at church. They talked and worked on sewing projects. Reading was also popular, but books were expensive. In the 1700s, one book cost $3. That would be worth about $66 today. To save money, people could join a subscription library. They paid one amount that let them borrow as many books as they wanted.

Wealthy women liked to shop. They bought cloth to make dresses, curtains, and cushions. Storekeepers would offer them tea and share the latest gossip.

Clothes

Wealthy people dressed in the latest fashions from **Great Britain.** Their clothes were made from expensive cloth that was made in other countries. They wore caps or, for parties or balls, tall wigs. Men's shirts and vests had silver buttons, and their shoes had buckles made of silver. Both men and women wore lace. People liked bright colors for clothes, such as red and blue.

GIRLS' FASHIONS

When Anna Green Winslow was ten years old, she went to Boston to live with her aunt. In her diary, she tells her mother that she does not want to wear her old black hat and red Sunday dress. She was afraid that people would think she was someone selling things on the street.

Hannah Babcock Bours was a very wealthy Massachusetts woman. In this 1759 painting, she is dressed in her finest clothes.

Workers and poor people wore clothes made of homemade cloth called homespun. Women wove the cloth out of yarn made from plant fibers. Most homespun was brown or gray because it was dyed with things like nutshells or plants. The buckles and buttons on their clothes and shoes were carved from wood.

At the time of the **Revolutionary War,** colonial leaders (on the left), workers, and servants (on the right), gather in a street. They are wearing the usual clothes of the 1760s.

Food and Drink

People ate roasted or boiled lamb, ham, or beef. Fish and oysters were popular, too. Breads were made from wheat and cornmeal. Wealthy people could pay for foods to be brought in from other countries, such as chocolate, lemons, almonds, raisins, and olives. Treats for poor or working people were molasses, maple sugar, apple butter, or pickles.

Fireplaces in colonial Boston often looked like this one. A kettle hangs over the fire. On the right are bellows to pump air into the fire, and scales to weigh ingredients for cooking.

Boston Recipe: Johnnycake

Tea was the most popular drink in the **colonies** until **Great Britain** put a **tax** on it in 1767. Because the tax also affected other foods, many people stopped drinking tea and eating foods that came from Britain. Johnnycake was a type of bread that **colonists** could make from local ingredients.

WARNING: Do not cook anything unless there is an adult to help you. Always ask an adult to help you use the oven and to handle hot foods.

YOU WILL NEED
1 cup (240 g) cornmeal
1/2 teaspoon salt
1 teaspoon sugar
1 cup boiling water
1 tablespoon butter
about 1 cup (240 ml) milk
a frying pan or griddle

FOLLOW THE STEPS
1. In a large bowl, mix together the cornmeal, salt, and sugar.

2. Pour in the boiling water and butter. Stir until blended. Let the mixture stand for about ten minutes.

3. When the mixture is puffy, stir in milk 1/4 cup (60 ml) at a time, until the mixture looks like mashed potatoes.
4. Drop onto a hot, buttered pan by tablespoonfuls.
5. Turn each cake once to brown on both sides.
6. Serve with butter.

23

Changes in Boston

People in Boston had copied **Great Britain** in their clothes, foods, homes, and hairstyles. But with every new law and **tax, colonists** grew angrier. What they ate, drank, and wore began to show their loyalty to their colony.

They stopped drinking tea that was brought in from Great Britain. They began having furniture and other goods made by local **craftspeople.** They began wearing clothes that were made of homemade cloth.

At meetings of the Sons of Liberty in early December 1773, the colonists worked out a plan to stop British ships from unloading tea in Boston Harbor.

Men formed groups such as the Sons of Liberty. They talked about how the **colonies** could make their own laws and gain their freedom. Women formed groups, too. A group called the Daughters of Liberty met at people's homes to make threads for homespun, sometimes spinning for twelve or fourteen hours at a time.

TAX DENIAL

Even wealthy women were against the taxes that Great Britain placed on the colonies. Newspapers throughout the colonies began to print notices by groups of wealthy women, called "ladies of quality." These notices announced that the women would no longer drink tea unless the situation was an emergency.

In Great Britain, magazine cartoons showed members of the British government crying over the loss of tax money from the colonies in North America.

Spreading the News

Printers in Boston played an important part in spreading the news about the struggle for **independence.** Printers **published** the laws for the **colonies.** They published accounts of what happened when groups like the Sons and Daughters of Liberty met. They also printed **pamphlets** containing people's ideas about independence.

At a printing press, pamphlets, posters, notices, newspapers, and broadsides were produced. They helped spread the news of **taxes** and of revolutionary meetings.

There were no photographs, but people could buy **prints** and political cartoons from printers. These pictures showed important events, such as the **Boston Massacre.** Printers helped get people to go to meetings. They printed large posters, called broadsides, and placed them around the city. All these things helped to turn the people of Boston against the British.

This broadside drawing by Paul Revere of the Boston Massacre did not tell the whole truth. It showed British soldiers shooting **colonists** who were protesting about the taxes. It made the colonists angry.

Boston Tea Party

On December 16, 1773, three ships full of tea sat in Boston Harbor. **Colonists** had been holding meetings about these ships all day. They did not want the tea, but the British wanted the tea unloaded and sold in the **colonies.** That night, a group of men dressed as Native Americans climbed onto the ships. In a few hours, they had opened all of the tea and dumped it into the water. This was the Boston Tea Party.

This 1846 painting shows the Boston Tea Party. After the event, it was hard for the people of Boston to get food and other things they needed. They had to have food and help from other colonies.

Things in Boston were never the same. The British were very angry. They sent ships to close the port. They put soldiers in people's homes.

News of the tea party traveled to the twelve other colonies. Soon, there were "tea parties" in other cities, such as Philadelphia and New York. The Boston Tea Party brought all the colonies together.

THE BRITISH LEAVE

Just two years after the Boston Tea Party, Boston was a changed town. More than 10,000 British soldiers lived there. Only 6,000 Bostonians still lived there. The fancy homes of wealthy merchants had been taken over by British officers. In 1776, Bostonians drove the British from their town for good.

British ships of war brought their soldiers into Boston Harbor. In 1774, British ships closed the harbor to colonial ships.

Boston Today

Today, nearly 600,000 people live in Boston. It is home to many museums, libraries, and colleges. Its port is one of the busiest in the world. Although tall buildings fill downtown Boston, visitors can walk on the Freedom Trail that leads them to the Old South Meeting House and Faneuil Hall. A **replica** of one of the Boston Tea Party ships has been made into a museum and is anchored in Boston Harbor.

The main square of Quincy Market is now on the Freedom Trail, which links all the historic buildings from the time of the **Boston Massacre,** the Boston Tea Party, and the **Revolutionary War.**

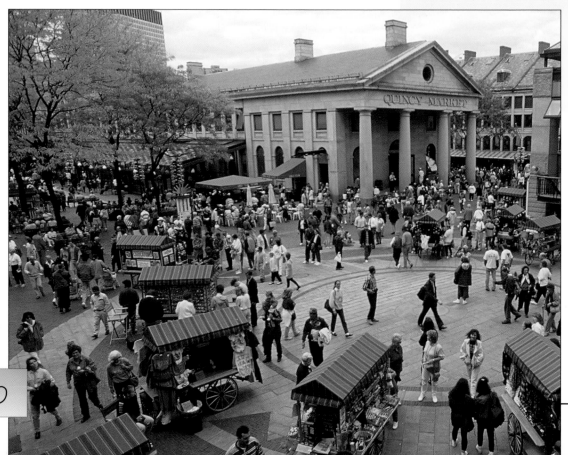

Glossary

apprentice person who lives and works with a craftsperson to learn a skill

Boston Massacre riot that happened in 1770, in which five people were killed

colonist person who lives in a place that is run by people from another country

colony new village, town or area that is set up in one country by people from a different country

craftsperson someone who makes things for a living, such as furniture, pottery, or clothing

Great Britain country formed in 1707 by England, Scotland, and Wales. The country is also called Britain and the people are called British.

immigrant person who moves from another country to live in a new country

Independence being free to do what one wants

pamphlet booklet

print picture made by putting ink on a design carved into wood or metal and then making copies on a printing press

publish to print a piece of writing and give it out to people

Puritan person who believed that church services should be simple and based on the teachings of the Bible

religion system of belief in a god or gods

replica something new made to look exactly like an old place or thing

Revolutionary War (1775–1783) war in which the North American colonies won independence from Great Britain

settler person who makes a new home in a new place

smuggling illegally bringing in or shipping out goods

tax money people must pay to the government

More Books to Read

Draper, Allison S. *What People Wore During the American Revolution.* New York: Rosen, 2001.

Erdosh, George. *Food and Recipes of the Thirteen Colonies.* New York: Rosen, 1997.

Wade, Linda R. *Life in Colonial America.* Minneapolis: Abdo, 2001.

Index